Victoria Plum

Victoria and the Lost Moonbeam

Angela Rippon

Illustrated by Colin Petty

Purnell

SBN 361 05579 X
Text copyright © 1983 Daredevils Limited.
Illustrations copyright © 1983 Purnell Publishers Limited.
'Victoria Plum' copyright © 1983 W.N. Sharpe Limited.
First published 1983 by Purnell Books, Paulton,
Bristol, BS18 5LQ, a member of the BPCC group.
Reprinted 1985.

Made and printed in Great Britain by Purnell and Sons
(Book Production) Limited, Paulton, Bristol.

Victoria's Magic Wish

Out in the Great Wood it was dark and cold, and nothing stirred. But inside the house of the woodland fairy Victoria Plum everything was bright and warm and cosy. Victoria and her friend Benjamin the elf were sitting in front of a cheery fire, having a feast of milk and biscuits. They'd both had a very busy day learning a new spell, and all around them on the floor, and on the tables, were piles and piles of fairy magic books. Their wise old teacher had said it was about time Victoria and Ben learnt one of the most important of all fairy

spells—how to grant three wishes. So they had spent the whole day reading their books and learning how to cast the spell.

"Do you think you've got the hang of it now, Ben?" asked Victoria.

"Well, I think so," said Ben. "Let me try it out on you. Only just ask for one wish, and don't make it too difficult."

"All right," said Victoria, and she began to think of a wish. "I wish," she said at last, "that I could have a pretty new hat."

"Why ever do you want a new hat?" said Ben.

"You've got at least six already."

"That's not the point," said Victoria, "this is supposed to be a wish, and that's what I want."

Ben knew it was useless arguing, so he closed his eyes tight, and tried to remember the right words for the spell. Victoria waited, and waited. But although her head did start to feel a little funny, her hat didn't change at all. At last Ben opened his eyes to see if the spell had worked. When he looked at Victoria he was horrified. "Oh dear," he said. "Oh dear, oh dear, oh dear." And then he burst into fits of giggles.

“What have you done?” said Victoria. But Ben was laughing too much to be able to answer her, so Victoria looked at herself in the mirror. She could hardly believe her eyes.

Ben’s spell hadn’t given her a new hat at all—it had given her new hair. Instead of her lovely thick dark curls, Victoria had bright green pigtails.

Ben was laughing so much that his sides ached. “Oh, you do look awful,” he said. And Victoria had to admit

that she did. It really was a particularly nasty shade of green. Then Victoria began laughing too. Fortunately, being a fairy, she knew she could put the spell right, so there was no point in being cross with Ben. At last Victoria said, "I don't think I like my new hat very much—so if you don't mind I'll magic the old one back again." With that she sprinkled her head with fairy dust, said a magic spell of her own, and the green pigtails disappeared. "That's better," said Victoria.

"Perhaps next time I'll just go and buy a new hat instead."

When Ben stopped laughing he said, "I am sorry, Victoria. And I think I'd better practise that spell a bit more before I try it out on anyone else—not everyone has your sense of humour." And Victoria agreed.

Ben looked out of the window. "My goodness it's dark," he said. "I didn't realise it was so late. I think I'd better be getting home."

He picked up his books, and after eating one last biscuit, he opened the front door and said goodbye to Victoria.

Outside the night was as black as coal.

Victoria and Ben's Discovery

Ben set off down the woodland path, but before he had walked twenty paces he heard Victoria calling him back. "Ben," she whispered, "I thought I heard a voice."

Together they peered into the dark, listening as hard as they could.

"There it was again!" she said, and out of the night came a faint whimpering.

Ben and Victoria followed the sound. "It's over here," said Ben. And there at the bottom of Victoria's garden, under one of the sleeping flowers, Victoria found a tiny moonbeam. She was curled up tight into a little ball, crying softly to herself.

"Please don't cry," said Victoria. "Can we help you?"

The little moonbeam was so pleased to see them both that she ran to Victoria and hugged her. "Oh, thank you for finding me," she said. "I was so frightened."

"But what were you afraid of?" said Victoria. "There's nothing to harm you here."

The little moonbeam looked very sorry for herself and said in a tiny voice, "I'm afraid of the dark."

"But that's impossible!" said Ben. "The moonbeams only come out when it's dark, so how can you possibly be frightened?" The moonbeam looked very unhappy, and said, "I know that all my sisters love the night. They dance and shine through the trees making everything bright with their lovely silver light. But tonight, when the dark clouds covered the moon, all my sisters went home, and I got lost." She sniffed and another large tear rolled down her tiny face. "I've never been on my own before," she said. "I'm too small to make a lot of light and everything seemed so dark. The trees were all whispering and moving around me like huge monsters, and I can hear all sorts of horrible noises. I was so frightened I just wanted to hide under this flower."

Ben was not at all impressed. "Silly thing!" he said. But Victoria felt sorry for the little moonbeam. She had lived in the Great Wood all her life. She knew every tree and flower, and all the animals and birds who lived there, and none of them were monsters. She also knew that many of the woodland creatures slept all through the day, and only got up at night. So Victoria had never been afraid of the dark because she was always surrounded by so many dear friends. "There really isn't anything to be afraid of," she said, trying to make the little moonbeam feel brave. "All the creatures in the wood are our friends and would never harm you."

But just then there was a mighty crash behind the hedge, followed by a loud snort, and a huge shadow loomed out of the night.

The little moonbeam screamed with fright, and clung to Ben for protection. Ben was so embarrassed he didn't know where to look.

The 'shadow' poked its nose round the hedge. "Evenin' all," it said, cheerily. Victoria recognised her visitor at once. It was Badger. He walked into the garden, sat down and said to the moonbeam, " 'ello. You're new here aren't you? Don't remember seeing you before."

Victoria explained that the little moonbeam had got

lost and was scared of the dark."

"And," she said, "you've just given her quite a fright crashing around in the wood like that."

"Oh dear me," said Badger, "now that is a shame. Sorry about that. Afraid of the dark are you? Well now, for myself, I much prefer the night. It's always so noisy during the day, with everyone dashing about. You can get a bit of peace and quiet at night time."

Now that the little moonbeam could see that Badger was quite harmless, and really very friendly, she sat down beside him and asked, "How on earth can you see where you're going in the dark?"

"See!" said Badger, outraged. "See!—what do you want to see for? I can smell everything I need to know. I can sniff out the best food, follow a track, and tell you who's been walking around. I can even tell you if it's going to rain. Oh yes—the nose is a wonderful thing you know. You ought to try and use yours a bit more."

The moonbeam sniffed the air. Badger smelt of warm fur and damp earth. It was quite a nice country smell really. "I'll remember that," she said, and smiled.

By now the moonbeam was beginning to feel quite brave again. But suddenly there was a swish in the air,

and a long, loud screech came echoing through the trees.

The poor little moonbeam nearly jumped out of her skin, and began shaking in her shoes.

"What was that?" she asked, shivering with fright.

But before Victoria could answer, Owl flew out of the darkness and settled on the ground like a cloud of white feathers, next to Victoria.

"Good evening, Miss Victoria," said Owl, who was always very polite. He then turned to the moonbeam and said, "I don't believe we've had the pleasure of meeting before." So Victoria explained that the moonbeam was lost, and that she was frightened of the dark.

Badger grunted and said, "I've already given her one fright tonight, and now you've just done it again."

The owl was most upset to think that he had frightened the moonbeam, so he looked at her with his wise old eyes and said, "I have never been afraid of the

dark, because my eyes are so bright that when I'm flying at night I can see as clearly as if it were the daytime. But I do understand that if you don't know the wood, then at night it could be a very scary place indeed, full of strange sights and sounds."

The moonbeam nodded—because she was still just a little too scared to speak.

Owl closed his eyes and put his head on one side. This meant that he was thinking about something very important. Owl was very old and very wise, and when he was thinking, he didn't like to be disturbed, so no

one in the garden dared say a word or move a muscle.

At last he opened his eyes and said, "I think I have a solution."

"Thank goodness for that," said Ben. But Owl gave him a stern look, so Ben stayed silent while Owl explained his plan.

Owl coughed—and began. "Victoria will cast a spell so that, just for tonight, you will be able to see in the dark as well as I can. Then I will carry you on my back, and we will fly through the wood together, and I will show you that there is nothing here to be scared of."

Victoria was delighted, because she knew that none of her magic was strong enough to make the moonbeam really brave, but she could easily manage a spell to make her see in the dark for a few hours. So Victoria said the magic words and sprinkled fairy dust on the moonbeam's eyelids.

The moonbeam blinked, then said, "My goodness—I really can see in the dark."

Owl spread his wings. "Come on," he said, "climb aboard, we're going on a flight."

The Midnight Flight

The moonbeam settled down into the warmth of the owl's feathers, and in a twinkling they were gliding off through the trees with Ben and Victoria flying behind.

In no time at all they saw the sleek red fox trotting

through the trees. "Hello, Fox," called Victoria.

The fox looked up and waved his long bushy tail at them. "Hello," he barked, "have a nice flight!" A little further on they saw the hedgehog snuffling through the leaves, and they heard him whistle with delight every time he found a tasty morsel to eat.

As they flew over a large clearing in the wood they suddenly saw the earth shudder and move. The next minute Mole poked his long nose into the night air, and gave a sniff.

"Hello, Mole," shouted Victoria.

"What?—oh—er—hello," said Mole, rather absent-mindedly. "Can't stop—have to finish this tunnel before morning," and he disappeared under-ground.

All night they flew through the Great Wood. They saw rabbits munching the grass on the river bank. There were mice playing hide and seek through the brambles, stoats hunting through the shadows, and bats squeaking with joy as they flew in and out of the branches of the high trees.

Owl was really enjoying his conducted tour. "You see," he said, "there's really nothing to be afraid of. The trees don't become monsters in the dark, and none of the animals will ever harm you."

At last they flew back to Victoria's garden where Badger was still waiting for them.

"Did you enjoy that?" he asked the moonbeam.

"Oh yes!" she said. "I don't think I'll ever be afraid of the dark again."

"Well that's all right then," said Badger.

"Pleased to be of service," said Owl.

And before anyone had time to say another word, they both disappeared back into the night.

Just then there was a rustle and scurry in the bushes.

This time the moonbeam wasn't at all afraid. Instead of shaking in her shoes, she went to see what had made the noise. A small mouse scampered out and almost fell over her feet. "Oh sorry," it said, "I appear to be lost."

The moonbeam smiled at him. "Don't worry," she said, "I just saw your brothers and sisters playing hide and seek in the wood. Would you like me to show you the way?"

"Yes please," said the little mouse, and he caught hold of her hand.

The little moonbeam was so happy that she glowed brighter than ever before. So that all the way home, although it was still dark, she and the mouse walked through the wood in a pool of silver light.

Once the little mouse found his brothers and sisters, the moonbeam raced back to Victoria's house.

"I did it—I did it!" she cried. "I walked in the dark all by myself, and I'm not afraid any more. Thank you so much, Victoria and Ben, for all your kindness."

At that moment the dark clouds moved away from the moon, and the rest of the moonbeams came tumbling down into the Great Wood. "Where have you been, sister?" they cried when they saw her. "You must come with us quickly, before the morning star lights up the sky."

The moonbeam ran to her sisters, but as she went she called back to Victoria and Ben, "Goodbye—I'll never forget you!" And as Victoria waved, she floated off into the darkness.

Ben gave a huge yawn. "Well," he said, "that's quite enough flying about for one night—I'm off to bed." And he flew off through the trees to his own house.

When Victoria was curled up in her own snug little bed, she looked through the window, hoping that she might see the little moonbeam again, but they'd all gone, so Victoria went to sleep.

But then a few days later something very strange happened. Although the wood was dark and the sky was as black as ink, there was a silver light over

Victoria's house. And that was when Victoria knew that the moonbeams had worked their own very special magic for her.

From that day, until forever, if anyone was lost in the Great Wood, they would always see the light over Victoria's house, and they need never be afraid of the dark again.